The Still and Fleeting Fire

by

Amina Alyal

&

Oz Hardwick

Here may indeed be torment, but not death.

—Dante Alighieri, *Purgatorio*, XXVII, 21

At a certain point, hopefully, we'll get back to a life

that is basically exactly the same as it was before.

However, we're quite a long way away from that at the moment.

—Prof Chris Whitty, BBC Breakfast, 11 January 2021

First published 2022 by The Hedgehog Poetry Press,

5 Coppack House, Churchill Avenue, Clevedon. BS21 6QW

www.hedgehogpress.co.uk

ISBN: 978-1-913499-48-8

Cover photographs © Oz Hardwick, Author photograph © Dave Gough

How different were these entryways from those

of Hell! For here it is with song one enters;

down there, it is with savage lamentations.

—Dante Alighieri, *Purgatorio*, XII, 112-4

for Karl Baxter

Contents

UP

Home is the place where dark is certified, stamped with more stars than we've yet named; where even the most trusted guides have nothing to offer but their experience of having been lost a million times before. Here, our boots are heavy with classical allusions, our clothes inappropriate for our unreliable memories, and even our conception of darkness is untrustworthy beneath the freshly illuminated Sun. Stairs become slopes, with terraces that track and tack their zigzag route to blue. *Up* is the only word that makes sense, and we repeat it like a mantra until it becomes nothing but rhythmical sound, and then nothing but circadian silence. Our self-appointed guide consults concordances and Google maps, checks endnotes and suggested further reading, then offers us mint cake and spring water. There's a song on the wind that pierces our insubstantial bodies, assuring us that home is where the heart never lies, and that if we can just keep putting one foot in front of the other, we'll be dancing before we know it.

ON THE VERGE

We have sewn our own eyes shut, so we don't see the bags of provisions going over the edge. Hordes of us lie, bereave(d of move)ment. We/they lie in half-lit rows of beds – too dim to walk any more – calling out, *Is this Hell?* Burdened, we climb the tiers. The giant sloth emboldens us to run, bearing leaden tons of gravity, away from the rising graphs, the ups and downs, the flat, flat lines. Rats come out of the woodwork but they don't carry plague, just the hope of a cleaner planet. So we race, staying in place, like the Red Queen, in this backwards game of bones. Weeping floods the streets, makes it dangerous to pass; half the roads are closed, the other half deserted. It's like house arrest, we/they say. It's lockdown. It's locking ourselves in with stitches we have applied ourselves, so we don't see the bags of fertiliser thrown over the edge. We don't want our bodies morphed by way of experiment, the way they do it in Hell. We don't want to eat morphed grain. We would rather starve, we/they say. But the ones that don't say, just starve. Who is left to farm when all of us are lying, heavy with boulders, our eyes sewn shut with our own needles, pecking up grain and adding it to the hoards we cover with our own bodies, climbing the tears? Angels arrive and we clap them but we/they don't pay for the service.

THE STATUES SPEAK

Until further notice, citizens should stoop. They should walk in circles with their opportunities and achievements distributed evenly across their shoulders for all to see. Those with sufficient voices should sing, and all should wear white gloves to clarify gestures of superiority, surprise, supplication, and the intrinsic sadness of the human lot. Tinted glasses may be worn, though corrective lenses are not permitted, and hearing trumpets may be utilised as long as all parties are in agreement. Parties and other intimations of community are forbidden. If animal familiars are unavoidable, lions may be employed, though they must be quarantined for an indeterminate period in order to prevent the spread of allegory. In case of mirrors, darkness should be employed. All emergency services are sleeping and should not be disturbed until the last cat wails.

SMUGGLING HOPE

Checkpoints bloom like bruises on every street corner and queues form hours ahead of every opening: shops, theatres, doctors' surgeries, and restored pleasure gardens redolent of an imagined Golden Age. I have hired a guide to smooth my passage; a laurel-crowned psychopomp steeped in The Knowledge, with palms slick with ready obols and greasy fivers, and the gift of the gab of a cocky Late-Repentant, with all the innocence misunderstanding brings. It's a steep climb to the midnight news and further still 'til morning, and there are pipers to pay, delays to wait out, and outriders to dodge on the winding path. I've taped my failings to my limbs and torso, poorly hidden beneath a loose suit, and I've a suspicious-looking suitcase bulging with McGuffins and red herrings borrowed from the plots of sixpenny pulps with lurid covers. My guide says we should hurry, but stops to hear the stories of each sinner that we pass, and when we finally reach the striped barrier at the front of the queue – when I glimpse for the first time white fountains, slim, kind-eyed beasts, and pendulous fruits fat on golden boughs – he's nowhere to be seen.

GNOMIC EQUIVALENCES

The Devil persuaded us he knew better than the seamstress, so we thread the whole bobbin at once. We have to walk endlessly round the block to get to the end, every day, pulling on that yarn as it snarls itself in weeds and catches at the stars. It would work if the yarn was always the same but its substance keeps changing and its reactions are not what we expect. We didn't realise it was so elastic and now our stitches are rucking at the cloth and we might have to do it all again. No one can understand what we are trying to stitch. But it's all OK because none of us casts a shadow and that's how we know we aren't real and hugs after all are plentiful, easy on the muscles when our arms pass through pixelated selves. The people we are watching smile and rage but they speak forever and so we realise they died last year. And now our guide is telling us it's significant that the gryphon tied itself to a tree and that's so hard to fathom that we pull out our tarot packs, tangling with the Lovers, the Empress and the Sun. The long twine is still there and it's the only thing holding us to our demarcated route, which is specified so that we get to know the local area. All around the Earth the mountains shake and we are no longer sure we are on solid ground. We say to each other, *During lockdown one of the forbidden things was singing but birds sang all the more.* The Devil has been three times round that tree and has ravelled his thread in one of the weeds at the foot of the telegraph pole and has given up because the tangle is too much, it's too much.

THE DUALITY OF AFTERTHOUGHT

Plucking at the sea, a retired pilot remembers when the sky was blue and plump for the plucking. Clouds were always fat and ripe, and he'd stuff them in the zip pockets of his cracked leather jacket, then hand them out to children who may or may not have been his. One smile at the edge of a new country and no one would ask him for papers or explanations, and even when he'd shrugged off his glamorous wings there were no repercussions or outstanding payments for daring airborne indiscretions. The sea was a mirror then, full length and fawning at every pose and manoeuvre; and often he'd take it in his arms at night and let it croon him to sleep, then wake him to an alarm of gulls and the smell of French coffee. He still goes there in his dreams, but now the sea is a one-string fiddle with a broken bow, a grey cloak that keeps neither cold nor birds at bay, a child that spits at its adopted father. His arm is a wave of decaying particles, his eyes sewn closed with iron wire.

THE LION NEVER SLEEPS

Lions in our eyes; afterimages of afterimages, red with the pressure of stories and grazed knuckles. One wrong word and everyone's King of the Beasts, squaring up to imagined slights with tooth, claw, and every scrap of fireside tales they can cram into an indignant roar. Thinking never got anyone anything but trouble, and the best defence is vigilance, ambush, sleight of hand, and the proverbial deep first cut. There are circumstances in which any of us may become stone, so a degree of amateur lithomancy doesn't go amiss; likewise, we may flare at the drop of a hint, so pyromancy's essential for a roll-out toolkit. Out of strength comes sweetness. The nearer the bone, the sweeter the meat. Revenge is sweeter before the first offence. A stone lion stares from a raging fire, its clear quartz eyes streaming with amplified tears of wrath and passion. All we can see are afterimages of afterimages. The King is dead, the king is red; long live smoke and funhouse mirrors.

ALLEGORY OF SHAME AND GUILT

We watch the angel go after the snake and the snake as it escapes from the garden. Must we be kind even to snakes? R is the letter stamped on our foreheads and we must never wash our hands in the wrong order or we have to start again. We must play hopscotch, we must say thank you or sorry if we forget; we should be ashamed of ourselves; we must shout slogans about liberty and send our saviours to Hell. Only frowns and narrowed eyes and laughter lines must be moulded, and that takes a lot of clay and sweat. We know how to be acrimonious, how to laugh, in these lachrymose times. We are the lost children of Eve. Or at least that's what we say, tired of trying to read body language when none of us casts any shadows. Time flexes itself in the stars, which can only be seen because they are dead, and because of this someone bares their breast and shows us a wounded heart, and all the ravening sheep wolf down that bleeding flesh. Forbidden to sing, forbidden to touch, we always feared the wolf, the lion and the boar. Now the wolf, the lion and the boar are our prey, and that means mercy and compassion but nevertheless it's the shrinking wild that caused all the trouble in the first place. I/we wonder what the planet is up to. Hope like a faint orange fox trots across the corner of the street, and these are the signs of fresher, fuller air.

BETWEEN THE ACTS

In the city between the cities, grey men stride with furled umbrellas and tablets weighted with figures. Pavements are grooved with heels and wheeled cases, and the breath of agitated buildings is stripped to ribbons by couriers' bikes weaving between time zones. In neon doorways, scrubbed bodies are stacked for sale, each cheaper than the last, knocked down and discounted into jangling change. Payments are grasped and double-entered by two-faced homunculi in starched collars and dark glasses, their two slit mouths spiralling into gyres of self-contradiction. *They're so small*, says someone who may be a reporter for the local news, though he may be just another man with a rolled umbrella and a tablet, playing the markets. Prayer mats are grouped in doorways hung with ribbons to discourage flies from landing on the bruised bodies that jostle in the breath of buildings, and grey women hoist their palms towards a rented, makeshift Heaven. For all the wheeling and dealing, the fuss and furore, in the city between the cities, we're only waiting. *They're so small*, says God or the Big Bad Wolf, packing his case with rescinded bills.

THE PRICE OF EVERYTHING

Glass towers reflect, dreaming of a city that only ever existed in half-light. In glass halls, traders in red braces and 80s haircuts scream themselves hoarse, like kids on a rattling switchback ride as it shakes them over the abysmal sea, while their glass wives, ordered from ads in the back of a lads' mag, glitter on garden terraces, decorous as expensive watches, with voices like popping corks. It's noon or midnight: someone's glass is half empty while another's is half full, just as someone's glass ceiling is another's glass dancefloor. Children are glass beads on anklets and abaci, bought and sold like shares in rare futures. At this altitude, air is rarefied, each breathable molecule weighed on the scales of a blind man's eyes. Glass fingers indicate a stained-glass wedding, blessing a market barker's beautiful daughter as she returns to sand in a bullish wide boy's fist.

REVOLUTION IN THE SYSTEM

We open all the doors and let the animals in. The air is full of particles – dust, cells, bacteria, viruses. We can see the thick soup we live in, and what it all boils down to is that we are just configured differently, for a while. Our impulses are all electric, and it makes our hair stand on end to discover we are specimens on an apothecary's shelf, trimmed into glass jars – just face and hands, no more – unreadably remote. We say inconsistently we don't believe in God, but someone sent us the plague. Perhaps it was us. They are saying now that particles exist in two places at once (*batter my heart, batter my heart*), that the philosopher examined the arrow, and that life and death and even time aren't what we think they are. If we could reach the stars when they really existed, we could come back and see primeval ferns. But at this moment in time sheep may safely rage, so long as your filters are on. We/they say there's no choice: well, ha, there isn't at this late stage. Are all the planets in a state of atrophy? Is work all there is? Is it all lies? Is there any news? How do liars look after their figures? Is it better to dance to a video or to go outdoors? Is there a virus outside, ravening like a Dire Wolf, breathing on the flimsy timber of our hearts?

AFTER THE SHOW

Trust fell from your fingers as you left the theatre, or maybe it slipped down the side of the seat as you turned to speak to someone just before the curtain rose. Perhaps it stuck to that crisp note in the taxi when you told the driver to keep the change, and he smiled because it was the best tip he'd had all night, and you had been his last fare, and he could turn off that yellow light at last and cross the Rubaconte back to the land of the living. Whatever the story, by the time you arrived, shoeless, in front of the midnight news, and watched those old white men painting themselves whiter, and listened to their tales of a high-speed train to the city beyond the endless cloud, you knew you had lost it forever. So, you phone your mother to listen to the reassurance of the dial tone, gentle as a sleeping cat; but, for the first time since she stepped onto that swaying punt, she answers. *Here may indeed be torment*, she says, *but not death.*

UNTO THE STARS

When the dream becomes flesh, it borrows someone else's face; a face that's older than I expected, and which stops me in my tracks with a beauty beyond clickbait, Beatrice, or even the Widow Wadman herself. She looks at me with eyes that may not see inside me – may not see me at all – but which hold everything I've been searching for since before I even knew there were things to be found. She speaks in the voice of compassion without concession, quietly demanding full confession, contrition, and the restitution of deeds. I have come a long way, yet still I'm nowhere. My erstwhile guide, my foul-weather friend, angles his phone in hope of a signal, lost without Google or GPS, then fades into the background. The dream takes my hand, and I remember our faces brushing over rarely read books; I remember a frozen carpark reflecting falling stars; I remember grey motorways devolving into green tracks fringed with dancing light. A blank fingerpost gestures towards the only road there is. We walk.

THE MEASURE OF ALL

The angels are all on furlough and we must bake our cakes along the way. We wear seven-league boots, but even then the effort is too great to travel more than one stretching, desiccating inch. Looking back we can see the span of a ruler; looking ahead there's no more than a furlong, but it seems as if it could possibly go on forever. There's not much in the garden this time of year but even that is going to rack and ruin. I/we can do it but it will take some pruning and airing. We have needle-felted our own earmuffs so that we don't have to listen to the screams. Our brains are not wired for this, and we can't understand how climbing a mountain is the way to purge our regional maps of blots and stains. Our hands and our faces stay at home. I was told yesterday that liberty is more important than saving lives. I was told that dogs can't do maths or form complete sentences but today the sentence seems much too harsh. We are like dogs in that respect. Gravity pulls on my flesh like a grave-yard ghoul, seriously clinging on. My flesh is weak. But I still wish we could understand space-time and overcome, even if it is only for now. We must bake and brew, and mend and fix, and crochet ourselves a new place to live.

QUALITY STREET

Our bodies are translucent, like wrappers from the caramels that we only buy on special occasions: Blood Moons, birthdays, temporary truces, and Days of the Dead. It's none of those occasions, but we've learned to take celebrations where we find them, and every day is a saint's day or an anniversary, with memories of martyrdom, public mourning, and TV specials with talking heads who weren't there but have seen enough clip shows to know what to say. A translucent child calls from the back of a passing car, but the trees that line the verges are talking too loudly to catch their meaning. We're all hungry here, our pockets full of nothing but empty wrappers. The sky melts like a glass question mark. When did our skin become so thin?

A MACHINE FOR MAKING CLOUDS

You maintain your devotions though angels are dead, their epitaphs written in ballpoint on café walls. Where once was prayer, now there's intertextuality, and you tell me about ringing bells and old men in big coats and wire spectacles; and it calls to mind shadowy doorways, garbled codewords, and brown briefcases exchanged beside iced lakes. *No,* you say, *look*; and you point to a snow-bound bridge across the Hudson, the Styx, or the Tamar, with two frozen figures listening to the river far below. One figure could of course be me or my father, while the other could be Mum's uncle who never recovered from the War. Bells ring and we both genuflect from habit, you considering the Holy Trinity and me dodging a stray bullet. *Look,* I say, and point to the neat letters on the wall. They're in my handwriting from when I was somewhere around seventeen, when ice cream vans called the faithful with rousing hymns, and when every stranger could be a spy. Back then I could have been someone, could have been a contender; and you could have been a singing nun or an angel.

STATISTICAL MYSTERIES

Get me a shirt from a house that Death has not visited. Soil falls off a spade. The body struggles beneath. Leaves and sunlight intersect with cut flowers on an unexcavated tell. I walk silent streets and still sunlit riverbanks. Second by second, stuff pours while we wait and watch, and then it dawns on me, light edging the darkness in ways I don't want to see, and here on my left side a telling scar glows phosphorescent, only there at night. Lost, forgotten folk peer in at the glass pane, misting it with fears. They crowd together, marvelling, asking *Who are you? Who are you?* But we forget that when we shout at us/them in the street and on tablets. If only we/they had visited more houses in search of that shirt; and if we only keep control of our faces and wash our hands three times every thirty-three minutes, then we can save our souls. There is no warmth. The sun is pale, brittle. Washing lines flaunt many shirts but their wearers are all numbers, carved in stone.

LAST HOUSE STANDING

Here is real, with its bare floorboards and browning rose petals swept to one side. The car on the driveway is a filigree cage, fluttering with billets-doux, and the open doors – of car, house, and every chest and closet – are settling wings. Storks circle, ready to spirit away unnecessary babies, and there's a crow on the cradle with a glint in his eye and a nosegay of forget-me-nots held lightly in his beak. Here is the place we've made with our bare hands, irresistible in its soft edges and stripped deceits; where every room is a bedroom and all curtains are blazing; and where even the jumble of salvaged clocks know better than to chime out of turn. I switch on the radio, and it's that scent everyone wore in the mid-90s. I switch on all the lights and they are a low windchime calling across a field dusted with morning mist. Here is the place we've built from words, with antonyms slotting perfectly into their own paradoxical negations, with just enough friction to burn the tiny distance between us.

LAST NIGHT IN PURGATORY

When I come to the place that reminds me of home, there's nothing left of me but light and fingerprints. I know that I've crossed deserts and seas, and that I've slept beneath stars and gilded ceilings, but I had to leave the details and distinctions at the last border crossing when the guard told me sadly that even my empty bags were too heavy to pass. I remember dragging my aching limbs up endless iron steps in order to see the ideal city pinned out below, but when I looked down, I was standing on a wooden stool in my parents' kitchen at the centre of a mandala of broken crockery. Likewise, I remember a guide in white robes and a laurel crown, a thin finger urging me into the labyrinth; and I remember warm, loving breath in the bathroom of a hotel that was nothing but a film set or a pop-up theatre; but when I blinked, I was on a double-decker bus passing a garden centre, a sex shop, and a crematorium. Behind me there is nothing but fingerprints and unreliable memories; in front of me is a door that changes colour in my own flickering light. I lost my keys, or dropped them from the back of a cross channel ferry, and there's barely enough of me left to ring the bell. Curtains twitch like a glitch in an awkward call, but there is no shuffling on the white and laurel tiles.

FARE WELL

Listen to the thin air, listen to the silence, silence with no machines. In a lifetime each person walks three times around the equator, my guide tells me, but my journey is my journal in these long strange days, one tale, travel and travail – trivial games, possibly, but then again, true. Foraging, farming, flattening, I can hear the tree-ish voice: *I'll eat you as you eat me.* And I will find Easter eggs inside each leaf. Dandelion was not my cup of tea but now even nettle is, and my salad is wild garlic and sorrel but my own garden I have not kept. This does not matter when we find ourselves, slithering through, out of our depth, suddenly breathing. We can sit here awhile, on this plateau, our new eyes splitting open to clusters of smooth colour thrusting out of wet brown leaves. The thin, clean air will fill with petrol fumes. We will not have time to sleep, as long-legged tasks race us to the edge. We will not enjoy the loss of threaded walks around our neighbourhood, finding a tiny wooden hut in the bole of a tree. Watching coots busy on waterlily leaves. Seeing a squirrel skitter its way up a tree. Going outside at midnight and addressing the full Wolf Moon. So long since we arrived in that ship of fools, lit by the shine of an angel. Time has stretched like a womb. It will snap back and shrink. We will sew over it new tapestries till even the human skin is hid.

THE LAST BORDER

The roads are blocked by snow and suspicion, by stray animals and blinkered political motives, and the clouds are so low that there's turbulence in motorway laybys. We queue like it's the Eastern Bloc in the early 70s, defined by brutalist architecture and hidden agendas, hungry for bread and new music. There are more things in heaven and earth than are dreamt of in our philosophy, but there are gaps on shelves where the basics used to be stacked: flour, rice, toilet rolls, and shovels. There's a drift of hope on the autobahn, and offers of aid from friendly nations, but nothing has the correct paperwork and fields are filled with lorries as far as the heart can imagine. As wire and hunger prick our flesh, we argue and plead like the tumbling Tower of Babel, herding stray animals into temporary pens lined with worthless banknotes and cancelled visas. Scientists predict new strains of bluebirds and deep distrust, and the roads are blocked by fallen stars and fallen angels. Cue the music and the closing credits. Please leave your ideals as you found them.

AFTERWORD

2021 marks the 700th anniversary of the death of Dante Alighieri. These 21 prose poems were written in a three-way conversation with Dante, who brought his experience of Purgatory to bear as he led us through this era in which we, too, find ourselves trudging an upward spiral with only hope to sustain us. As in his celebrated journey, we encountered trials and obstacles to overcome and lessons to learn, and his guidance was invaluable. We hoped that he would show us Paradise but, like his Roman predecessor, he could only take us so far, leaving us with Virgil's valediction: *You have seen the temporary fire and the eternal fire; you have reached the place past which my powers cannot see.* The next step is ours to choose.